PUBLIC PROPERTY

T0353309

For my parents, Mick and Barbara

Sam Peter Jackson

PUBLIC PROPERTY

OBERON BOOKS
LONDON

First published in 2009 by Oberon Books Ltd
Electronic edition published in 2013

Oberon Books Ltd
521 Caledonian Road, London N7 9RH
Tel: +44 (0) 20 7607 3637 / Fax: +44 (0) 20 7607 3629
e-mail: info@oberonbooks.com
www.oberonbooks.com

A catalogue record for this book is available from the British
Library.

PB ISBN: 978-1-84002-977-2
E ISBN: 978-1-78319-367-7

Cover photograph by Graham Michael.

eBook conversion by Replika Press PVT Ltd, India.

Characters

GEOFF
Late 40s/early 50s, well respected
popular newsreader

LARRY
Late 30s/early 40s, Geoff's publicist

JAMIE
16, Northern teenager

Public Property was first presented by Tara Wilkinson on behalf of Whippet Productions at the Trafalgar Studios on 10 November 2009 with the following cast:

GEOFF, Robert Daws

LARRY, Nigel Harman

JAMIE, Steven Webb

On-screen cast:

HARVEY MILLNER, Stephen Fry

TV PRESENTER, Natasha Little

REPORTER, Elize du Toit

Director Hanna Berrigan

Designer Helen Goddard

Lighting Designer Emma Chapman

Sound Designer Steve Mayo

Productions

Act One

SCENE 1

A bare stage with a large television, which is showing a montage of moments from a news programme. Short excerpts of serious news stories and of more trivial entertainment and celebrity stories are rapidly intercut with moments of static, underscored by slightly unsettling music. The newsreader in all excerpts is GEOFFREY HAMMOND, a well-dressed, clean-cut man in his late 40s/ early 50s.

GEOFF: (*On TV.*) Good evening… (*Static.*) …good evening… (*Static.*) …good evening… (*Static.*) …tonight's headlines… (*Static.*) …headlines… (*Static.*) …Downing Street has revealed… (*Static.*) …a vote in the House of Lords on Monday… (*Static.*) … in which 20 people were injured… (*Static.*) …the Royal Family has refused to comment… (*Static.*) …good evening… (*Static.*) …and finally… (*Static.*) …a school in Cheshire… (*Static.*) …to honour Britain's oldest working single mother… (*Static.*) …came second in the popular reality show… (*Static.*) …the actress revealed her secret was regular exercise and… (*Static.*) …good evening… (*Static.*) …jailed in Los Angeles for violating a probation on a driving ban… (*Static.*) …an apology over the telephone voting scam… (*Static.*) …good evening… (*Static.*) …and finally… (*Static.*) …good evening… (*Static.*) …and finally… (*Static.*) …good evening… (*Static.*) …and finally… (*Static.*) …and finally.

Disturbing music plays as the camera zooms into GEOFF's face until we can only see the pixelation of the TV. Sudden cut of sound and lights.

SCENE 2

Exclusive London restaurant. GEOFF and LARRY are sitting at a table, looking at their menus.

GEOFF: So?

LARRY: So what?

GEOFF: So how are the reviews?

LARRY: Relax, let's eat first.

GEOFF: Why?

LARRY: We've got plenty of time.

GEOFF: Just tell me.

LARRY: Take it easy, let's have a chat, drink some wine, enjoy the food…

GEOFF: OK.

LARRY: Great. Things alright with Paul?

GEOFF: Yes, great, thanks.

LARRY: Elaine giving you any trouble?

GEOFF: No, she's getting half of the money. That's all she ever wanted anyway.

LARRY: In return for waiting another year.

GEOFF: Yes, well, just until I've finished the tour and the documentary has gone out.

LARRY: And Paul's fine with that?

GEOFF: Yes.

LARRY: He won't give us any trouble?

GEOFF: What do you mean?

LARRY: He understands?

GEOFF: Yes, he understands.

LARRY: You want me to draw up a contract?

GEOFF: I'm not gonna get my boyfriend to sign a confidentiality agreement. He's made enough sacrifices already.

LARRY: Hey, I'm just checking, that's what I'm here for.

GEOFF: It's not easy for him as it is.

LARRY: I understand. Just trying to help.

GEOFF: Sure.

LARRY: What are you in the mood for?

GEOFF: Sorry?

LARRY: To eat.

GEOFF: I don't know. What's good here?

LARRY: The steak's good. They have it imported from Argentina. All organic, free-range, corn-fed, what-do-you-call-it from well-adjusted cows in stable relationships.

GEOFF: What are you having?

LARRY: I might go for the curry.

GEOFF: Why are you making it so mysterious?

LARRY: I just fancy a curry.

GEOFF: No, the reviews.

LARRY: What?

GEOFF: Why are you making them so mysterious?

LARRY: I'm not making them mysterious.

GEOFF: Yes, you are.

LARRY: No, I'm not.

GEOFF: Yes, you….OK,…fine..

LARRY: I just want you to be in the right mood.

GEOFF: My mood's perfect…I don't know why…but hey, fine… I can wait…

LARRY: Great.

Pause. They stare at each other for a moment, then look at their menus again.

GEOFF: That good?

LARRY: Sorry?

GEOFF: Are they that good?

LARRY: Look….

GEOFF: OK, OK, OK…

Silence.

Shall we get some wine?

LARRY: Yes, if you want.

GEOFF: Or should that be champagne?

LARRY: Sorry?

GEOFF: Should I order champagne?

LARRY: If you want.

GEOFF: Would you like some?

LARRY: Champagne doesn't really agree with me.

GEOFF: Wine then…

LARRY: Yes.

GEOFF: A nice bottle of wine.

LARRY: Yes.

GEOFF: To…erm…celebrate?

LARRY: What?

GEOFF: To celebrate?

LARRY: Look, stop it, OK?

GEOFF: OK, OK, OK…

LARRY: You're building it up too much.

GEOFF: You're the one who won't tell me!

LARRY: I'd simply prefer to talk about it after dinner.

GEOFF: Why can't we do it now?

LARRY: I just want you to see them in context.

GEOFF: Why do I need to see them in context?

LARRY: So you don't misread them.

GEOFF: What would I misread?

LARRY: Well, you know how it is. Sometimes it's easy to read too much into a flippant remark or a minor criticism.

GEOFF: So there's criticism?

LARRY: I didn't say that…

GEOFF: (*Interrupts.*) Minor criticism. You said there was minor criticism.

LARRY: I was being hypothetical.

GEOFF: So there's no criticism?

LARRY: Yes…No!…Well, of course there's some…Look…

GEOFF: So what? The reviews are…mixed?

LARRY: Can we talk about this later?

GEOFF: OK. Fine. But there's nothing to be worried about, right?

LARRY: No. There's nothing…there's nothing we can't sort out.

GEOFF: Sort out?

LARRY: Yes.

GEOFF: Sort out? What? Like the Mafia sort things out?

LARRY: I mean we can address the problem.

GEOFF: Problem?

LARRY: ISSUE!! We can address the issue!

GEOFF: What fucking issue?

LARRY: I'll tell you later!

GEOFF: You can't say that there's an issue and then not tell me…

LARRY: I am gonna tell you. I just think it's better if we…

GEOFF: Oh for fuck's sake, Larry. Will you stop treating me like a child?!

LARRY: Just wait, OK??!!

GEOFF: How are the reviews, Larry? Tell me, I'm a big boy.

LARRY: Christ!

GEOFF: I can take it, Larry. I've been reviewed all my adult life. I just want to know how they are, Larry. How are the fucking reviews??

LARRY: I just think it's better if we…

GEOFF: HOW ARE THE FUCKING REVIEWS!?

LARRY: BAD!!! VERY VERY BAD!!!

Silence.

They think your book is shit, shallow, vain, pretentious, smug and self-indulgent. They think a child of three with the brain of a retarded pig could have done better. They think you set the standard for a celebrity biography so low that it would qualify Victoria Beckham for a Pulitzer. And they generally think it's very very bad!

LARRY stares at GEOFF in silence. GEOFF is stunned. LARRY looks at his menu.

I think I might go for the fish.

Silence.

GEOFF: So there's not one that thinks it's…

LARRY: Nope.

GEOFF: So everyone thinks it's…

LARRY: Bad?

GEOFF: Uh-huh.

LARRY: Yah.

GEOFF: So there's…

LARRY: Not a single fucking quote for the paperback.

GEOFF: Shit.

LARRY: I know

GEOFF: Shit. Shit.

LARRY: I'm sorry, Geoff.

GEOFF: Shit. Fuck. Shit.

LARRY: Look, reviews aren't everything. Sales might still be good. We can address this.

GEOFF: I don't understand.

LARRY: We've got a few editorial pieces coming up…

GEOFF: Why couldn't you wait until after dinner? I was in such a good mood.

LARRY: What?

GEOFF: How could this happen?

LARRY: The book tour will make a big difference. You'll still sell in the provinces.

GEOFF: How could you let this happen?

LARRY: The thing with...what did you say?

GEOFF: How could you let this happen?

LARRY: Me? I get coverage and publicity. That's what I do. I'm not a journalist.

GEOFF: Bad publicity? Is that what you do? Get people bad publicity?

LARRY: No publicity is bad publ....

GEOFF: Oh, don't give me that PR textbook bullshit!

LARRY: I have got you coverage in every national newspaper...

GEOFF: And you can't get one of them to say something nice about me? What fucking good is that gonna do?

LARRY: If they don't like the book, that's not my responsibility.

GEOFF: Bullshit! You told me we had nothing to worry about. You said you had relationships with these people. That they wouldn't fuck us over.

LARRY: Their opinion is their opinion, that's out of my control.

GEOFF: Couldn't you bribe them?

LARRY: That wouldn't work.

GEOFF: What about the tabloids?

LARRY: That would work, but we don't have the budget.

GEOFF: I just don't understand how you could have let this happen! This is your responsibility, your fucking job!

LARRY: I don't write reviews, Geoff. But let me tell you what I do. I snap one finger and you become bedtime reading for every book reviewer in London. I snap two fingers and they print a massive airbrushed picture of your fat face in every national newspaper. I'm the best in the business. Because I've done my homework. So maybe next time you might want to consider writing a better book. *That* might get us a little further.

Silence.

GEOFF: (*Suddenly calm and collected.*) Well, Larry, I do my homework too. And when I first hired you, I did so because you *were* the best in the business.

But that was three years ago. And as we're being frank, I'm sure you won't mind me saying that your current reputation is that of a cokehead bullshitter who needs more hits than Google to get him through the day, and whose high-profile clients are jumping ship faster than you can say 'iceberg ahead'.

So I thought I wouldn't be like the others. I thought I'd give you a chance to go back to the glory days. And that I would be rewarded for my loyalty. But you let me down.

I know about the debts, the drugs, being dropped from your little programme.

I even know that the car parked outside this restaurant has been rented for the day to impress me. Unfortunately liars don't impress me, Larry.

You're fired. Your contract will terminate a month from today.

So I suggest you snap those two fingers, and take the third out of your arse and snap that one too.

Silence.

I think I'll have the steak.

SCENE 3

Car park outside Geoff's hotel, night.

JAMIE is standing in a dimly lit car park outside a hotel somewhere in the North of England. He is wearing a hoodie and seems slightly nervous. GEOFF enters.

JAMIE: Excuse me?

GEOFF: Yes?

JAMIE: You're on that show, aren't you?

GEOFF: Sorry?

JAMIE: You're on that show.

GEOFF: The news…?

JAMIE: Yes, that's the one. What's your name?

GEOFF: Geoff.

JAMIE: I mean your full name.

GEOFF: Hammond. Geoffrey Hammond.

JAMIE: Oh yeah. Geoffrey Hammond – *News at Ten.*

GEOFF: Yes.

JAMIE: That's you.

GEOFF: Yes, that's me.

JAMIE: You're really famous, aren't you?

GEOFF: Well, I guess you could say so.

JAMIE: Rich and famous. Is that your car?

GEOFF: (*nervously.*) Erm…Yes.

JAMIE: That's a nice car.

GEOFF: Thanks.

JAMIE: What is it?

GEOFF: Erm…It's a BMW M6 Convertible.

JAMIE: Nice. You must be really rich.

GEOFF: Look, I'm not carrying any valuables. I have a bit of cash in the car. I can be very cooperative.

JAMIE: You what?

GEOFF: I wouldn't press charges.

JAMIE: You think I wanna rob you?

GEOFF: Well…

JAMIE: You think all Northern teenagers are criminals?

GEOFF: No, sorry…

JAMIE: I was just having a bit of a chat…

GEOFF: Sorry, I didn't mean to…

JAMIE: Just because I'm not Southern and famous doesn't mean I'm scum.

GEOFF: I'm really sorry. I misread the situation.

JAMIE: You misread the situation? You shouldn't make assumptions about people like that.

GEOFF: I know. I'm sorry.

JAMIE: Stuff like this always happens to me. It's just so hard when you try to be a nice person, but life still always slaps you in the face. I just can't take it anymore …

JAMIE cries.

GEOFF: Oh, shit. Please don't cry.

JAMIE: I'm sorry. I can't help it. It just all gets too much for me sometimes. People are just so judgemental all the time.

JAMIE cries even louder.

GEOFF: Please. Keep it down just a little bit. I'm really sorry to have upset you.

JAMIE: (*Calming down.*) It's alright. It's not your fault. I'm sorry, I feel really stupid now.

GEOFF: Don't.

JAMIE: You're like the most famous person I've ever met and I'm making a complete tit of myself.

GEOFF: It's OK. Relax. Is there anything I can do?

JAMIE: No, I'll be alright. What you doing up here anyway?

GEOFF: I'm staying at the hotel. I'm on a tour.

JAMIE: Oh. You in a band?

GEOFF: No, a book tour.

JAMIE: What do you do on a book tour?

GEOFF: Well, I just go to bookshops around the country and sign copies of my book.

JAMIE: Isn't that a bit dull?

GEOFF: Well, yes. It can be.

Uncomfortable silence.

JAMIE: Can I have your autograph?

GEOFF: Erm...that might be a bit weird now.

JAMIE: No, go on.

GEOFF: Well, OK.

JAMIE: I'm gonna show my mates that I got Geoffrey Hancock's autograph.

GEOFF: Hammond.

JAMIE: Yeah.

GEOFF: I've got a pen. Have you got something to write on?

JAMIE: No, just write it on my arm.

GEOFF: OK.

JAMIE: Could you make it out to my sister?

GEOFF: But it's on your arm.

JAMIE: Oh yeah, I didn't think about that. Well, just make it out to me then.

GEOFF: What's your name?

JAMIE: Jamie.

GEOFF: Jamie.

GEOFF writes on JAMIE's arm. JAMIE looks at it.

JAMIE: (*reading.*) 'To Jamie. Lots of love, Geoffrey Hammond'.

GEOFF: Yeah.

JAMIE: Lots of love, eh?

GEOFF: Well, that's just what I write.

JAMIE: In your book?

GEOFF: Yes, in my book. Actually my contract says that I'm only allowed to sign my autograph in my books, so that one's extra special.

JAMIE: Thank you.

GEOFF: You're welcome. Well, I'm sorry again about before.

JAMIE: Don't worry.

GEOFF: I'll say goodnight then. Will you be alright?

JAMIE: Yeah.

GEOFF: Are you sure there's nothing I can do?

JAMIE: Well,…I'd love a ride in your car.

GEOFF: Oh…erm…OK.

JAMIE: Oh, I shouldn't have asked, should I?

GEOFF: No, it's fine.

JAMIE: Are you sure?

GEOFF: Yeah.

JAMIE: That's really generous of you.

GEOFF: It's no problem.

JAMIE: Thanks. (*Beat.*) I like *generous* older men.

SCENE 4

Interior, living room, LARRY's house, Night. Darkness. A phone is ringing. LARRY enters. He switches the light on. The house is small, modern, designer, luxurious, but a little chaotic and could probably do with a good clean. The room is split into two levels. The front level is slightly lower. The front door is in the middle of the back wall, there is little table with a telephone and a window to the left of it. There is a door stage right, which leads to the bedroom and the bathroom, and another door stage left, which leads to the kitchen. On the front level there is a three-piece suite with a table and a television, as well as a desk with a laptop and a chair. LARRY is wearing a T-shirt and a pair of sweatpants. He puts his glasses on and stumbles to the phone.

LARRY: Yes! For fuck's sake.

He answers the phone.

Hello?…Yes, of course I was…Why would I be up at 4 in the morning?…OK, 5 then, why would I be up at 5?…What?…When was this?…What an idiot! What a fucking idiot!…Sorry, Cindy. I know you don't like it when I…Yes, I know, there's a nicer way of expressing the same thing…What a cunt! Is he fucking insane?…Well, this isn't my problem anymore…Have you spoken to him? Have you…He's not picking up?…Where's he now?…Where would he drive to at this time of night?

The doorbell rings.

Shit. Cindy, I'll call you back…Honey, I'm a publicist, not a fucking magician…

LARRY hangs up the phone. Loud knocking at the door. LARRY tries to ignore it, but can't. GEOFF speaks to him through the letterbox in LARRY's door.

GEOFF: (*Off.*) Larry, let me in.

LARRY: Fuck off!

GEOFF: (*Off.*) Let me in!

LARRY: No!

GEOFF: I can see you, Larry! They're fucking following me! Let me in!

Reluctantly LARRY opens the door. GEOFF enters.

Do you want to kill me?

LARRY: With every bone in my body!

GEOFF: They're following my car!

LARRY: Are you drunk?

GEOFF: I've not had very much.

LARRY: Enough to smell drunk.

GEOFF: I'm not drunk!

LARRY: I didn't say you were drunk. I said you smell drunk.

GEOFF: You've heard?

LARRY: Cindy called me.

GEOFF: Shit. Cindy knows?

LARRY: Of course she fucking knows.

GEOFF: I never knew you wore glasses.

LARRY: I never knew you fucked around with kids, it's just a night of new discoveries.

21

GEOFF: Don't start on that one. He's not a kid. He's 16. 16 is legal.

LARRY: Yes, in some countries it is.

GEOFF: It's legal here. It's perfectly legal in this country.

LARRY: That's beside the point.

GEOFF: Gay men have fought for this right.

LARRY: To fuck teenagers in cars?

GEOFF: God, you look a mess. What's with the boxes?

LARRY: My sister's stuff. She's going through a divorce. Don't change the subject!

GEOFF: Do you have any orange juice?

LARRY: What?

GEOFF: Do you have any orange juice?

LARRY: Listen to me. You are in deep shit, Geoff. If you drag me down with you, I will make your life a living hell, do you understand? And no, I don't have any fucking orange juice.

GEOFF: Don't they say that? If you drink a pint of orange juice you won't have a hangover in the morning.

LARRY: A hangover is gonna be the least of your worries in the morning!

GEOFF: It's legal. I've not done anything wrong!

LARRY: True. Apart from adultery, sex in a public place, driving under the influence and posing for some slightly unfortunate photographs it's all been totally fucking kosher!

GEOFF: I know you can turn this around.

LARRY: Get the fuck out of my house.

GEOFF: How dare you Larry! You are under contractual obligation to help me!

LARRY: You terminated that contract.

GEOFF: It's valid for another week and a half!

LARRY: Fuck you, Geoff.

GEOFF: We can go ahead and draft a new one right now.

LARRY: I'm not interested.

GEOFF: You need me. Your business depends on me. I'm...

LARRY: A loose fucking cannon, that's what you are.

GEOFF: I'll double your salary.

LARRY: No.

GEOFF: You can have a down payment now. I've got some cash on me.

LARRY: I don't want your dirty whore-money, Geoff. You come here, get me out of bed, probably lead the fucking paps to my door like the pied piper...

GEOFF: Don't worry, I shook them off about 2 miles from here.

In that moment there are sudden camera flashes from all windows, shouting and loud banging at the door.

Shit!

LARRY: Close the curtains! Close the fucking curtains!

They run around the apartment frantically closing all the curtains, locking the door, etc. – greeted by flashes and shouting at every window.

(*Out of breath.*) You fucking idiot!

GEOFF: Let's stay positive.

LARRY: Positive?

GEOFF: Well, I thought we needed some extra publicity for the book.

LARRY: Lorraine fucking Kelly! Not this!

GEOFF: You should see this as your chance, Larry.

LARRY: My chance?

GEOFF: Turn this around and every celebrity in the country will be queuing for your services in the morning. It's a fantastic opportunity!

LARRY: You were caught with a young boy in…

GEOFF: He's not a young boy. He's 16. 16 is legal! Perfectly legal!

LARRY: NOT if you're paying!

GEOFF: I didn't pay.

Silence.

Much.

LARRY: Good night, Geoff.

GEOFF: You need me, Larry! You fucking need me!

LARRY: No, Geoff. I do not need you, I do not need this *fantastic opportunity* and I certainly don't need every backstreet weekend semi-paedophile to be queuing for my services in the morning. So thanks for the offer, but no thanks. Because when you hang yourself with this – and believe me, you will – I'll be in the front row sipping champagne.

GEOFF: I thought champagne didn't agree with you.

LARRY: Don't be here when I wake up. Or I'll call the police.

Silence. LARRY turns and makes his way to the bedroom.

GEOFF: Double salary and I take care of all your debt! Half now and half at the end of the tour.

LARRY stops and turns. They stare at each other in silence for a few moments. Then LARRY walks away into the bedroom and closes the door behind him. GEOFF is stunned. He runs to the door.

Don't do this to me, Larry. Please. Please don't do this.. I fucked up, Larry. I'm sorry. All these years of working together, they must mean something. They must give me at least some permission to fuck up every now and then. I'll do anything you want. Anything.

GEOFF gives up his pleading and gently sobs for a moment. Suddenly the bedroom door opens and LARRY comes out. He is now fully dressed in a sharp suit and ready for business.

LARRY: Stay where you are.

LARRY opens the front door to a lightning storm of flashing cameras. He walks out and suddenly snaps into performance mode. The door is left open. We cannot see the crowd, but we can see the back of LARRY with a bright light in front of him presumably coming from some of the TV cameras.

LARRY: Ladies and Gentlemen of the press, good morning. For those of you who don't know me, my name is Larry DeVries, I'm Mr Hammond's publicist. As you will appreciate, my client is in a very emotional state and needs some time to reflect upon these recent events. So if you could give us just a little bit more of your patience, we will do our best to have a statement ready for you within the hour. I won't be taking any questions at this time. Thank you for your cooperation.

He comes back in and closes the door. The cameras flash again.

Where's a fucking box of sample copies when you need them?

GEOFF: Thank you, Larry.

LARRY: Just so we're clear, I'm doing this for the money.

GEOFF: I understand.

LARRY: Let's get to work. Turn my computer on.

GEOFF: OK.

GEOFF turns the laptop on.

LARRY: I need to know every single detail of what happened tonight. Locations, positions, descriptions. We can't have any surprises in the early editions. I need complete honesty. Is that clear?

GEOFF: Of course, anything you want.

LARRY: Great. What time did you meet the boy?

GEOFF: Around 12.30 I think. I'd left my diary in the car and I went out to get it.
He was outside the hotel. He recognised me.

LARRY: What did you talk about?

GEOFF: It was all very strange. I thought he wanted to mug me.

LARRY: Mug you?

GEOFF: Yes.

LARRY: This young kid?

GEOFF: He's not a young kid. He's a teenager.

LARRY: Why did you think that he wanted to mug you?

GEOFF: Well, you know how threatening they can seem.

LARRY: Teenagers?

GEOFF: Yes. It was dark. He was wearing a hoodie. He was Northern.

LARRY: Northern?

GEOFF: Yes, Northern…You know, from the North.

LARRY: What's that got to do with it?

GEOFF: Well, certain accents can just sound a bit…threatening.

LARRY: Northern?

GEOFF: Yes. Well, you know how some of them talk.

LARRY: You're not gonna say this kind of thing in interviews, are you?

GEOFF: Of course I wouldn't! I'm just saying…

LARRY: Northerners don't sound threatening. Banks use them for voice-overs.

GEOFF: I'm just saying there are certain things that create threatening associations.

LARRY: Right.

GEOFF: Like if he'd been black.

LARRY: You're definitely not gonna say that in interviews, are you?

GEOFF: That's not racist. Statistically they're just more likely to attack you.

LARRY: Or that. Right?

GEOFF: No, of course I wouldn't! I was just explaining why I thought he wanted to mug me.

LARRY: Because he was Northern?

GEOFF: Yes. And in a hoodie.

LARRY: Of course. In a hoodie. And black.

GEOFF: No, he wasn't black. I just said that as an example.

LARRY: Oh right.

GEOFF: That black people seem threatening.

LARRY: Will you stop saying that!

GEOFF: Fine fine fine. You know what I mean.

LARRY: So that was the attraction?

GEOFF: What?

LARRY: A bit of rough?

GEOFF: No. It was a complete misunderstanding.

LARRY: How can sex be a misunderstanding?

GEOFF: He didn't want to mug me. He…

LARRY: He was cruising you?

GEOFF: Not really. It got a bit weird. He started to cry and…

LARRY: You made him cry?

GEOFF: No, I didn't make him cry. He…

LARRY: He just burst into tears for no apparent reason?

GEOFF: Will you stop interrupting me?! He seemed sort of…lost. I felt sorry for him, he was kind of sweet, almost child-like…

LARRY: Child-like?

GEOFF: Innocent! He had a sweet, funny, child-like innocence.

LARRY: A child-like innocence?

GEOFF: Like a grown-up can have! Christ, I feel like I'm on trial!

LARRY: I didn't say anything.

GEOFF: You were doing a thing.

LARRY: I was repeating what you said. A child-like innocence.

GEOFF: Like an 85 year-old can have. Like when they stay young at heart. Like people when they get older and they revert to childhood.

LARRY: But he's not an 85 year-old. He doesn't need to revert to anything. He's already there.

GEOFF: He had an older energy.

LARRY: I thought he was child-like.

GEOFF: The energy of someone older who has…stayed young.

LARRY: And who looks young. And acts young. And is actually young as well.

GEOFF: Very funny!

LARRY: What happened then? After the…'misunderstanding'.

GEOFF: You're doing it again!

LARRY: What?

GEOFF: That sarcastic thing when you repeat something.

LARRY: I'm just clarifying what you said.

GEOFF: OK OK OK…Well, we talked for a bit and he asked if he could have a ride in my car.

LARRY: The ride of his life, no doubt.

GEOFF: That was the last thing on my mind! We drove around for a bit, then we parked in this layby. He started being quite flirtatious. He was the one making all the moves.

LARRY: Nobody's going to believe that.

GEOFF: Oh, why not? Because a young guy wouldn't go for someone like me?

LARRY: Because 16 year-old kids don't get their rocks off over grey-haired overweight men.

GEOFF: Well, this one did.

LARRY: What's he got? A fucking Santa Claus complex?

GEOFF: Look, believe it or not, he went for me.

LARRY: Because he's a money-grabbing whore!

GEOFF: Because we had a connection. For ages we just talked.

LARRY: Did you ask him what he wants for Christmas?

GEOFF: Fuck off! He told me that he'd made some plans, but was now having some financial difficulties.

LARRY: Plans?

GEOFF: Saving up to go to university in a couple of…

LARRY: Hang on.

GEOFF: What?

LARRY: University?

GEOFF: Yes, I said university! Will you stop repeating everything back!

LARRY: No no no. That's good.

GEOFF: What?

LARRY: That's the first useful thing you've said all night.

GEOFF: What do you mean?

LARRY: Find the positive in the negative! He was saving up for university. So he's not just some street-hustling whore. He's an aspiring academic trapped in a system of greed and commerce. Write that down.

GEOFF: Brilliant. Maybe we could say I was making a statement about tuition fees.

LARRY gives GEOFF a look.

Maybe not.

GEOFF types something into the computer.

LARRY: So you gave him the money to help with his studies?

GEOFF: Yes.

LARRY: How much?

GEOFF: A hundred quid.

LARRY: That won't even get him a cab to campus.

GEOFF: Well, I wasn't gonna pay for all of it, was I?

LARRY: Obviously not.

GEOFF: He was very appreciative.

LARRY: Obviously.

GEOFF: I didn't mean that! That just…sort of happened.

LARRY: After you gave him a hundred quid.

GEOFF: Yes, after that.

LARRY: What an unbelievable coincidence.

GEOFF: Well, I guess he wanted to…thank me.

LARRY: What happened next?

GEOFF: We'd only been at it for about 2 minutes or so when I spotted a photographer hiding behind a fence. I panicked and he noticed that I'd seen him. Then all of a sudden loads of them appeared. They came running towards the car. Lights flashing everywhere. I didn't know what to do. I mean what do you do first? Run away or check that you're decent?

LARRY: You check that you're decent.

GEOFF: Yes, I know that now! I just drove off. I wanted to get out there as quickly as I could. Then I hit one of the photographers.

LARRY: What?!

GEOFF: With my car.

LARRY: You hit one of the photographers with your car?

GEOFF: Yes. Cindy didn't tell you?

LARRY: No.

GEOFF: I ran into him by accident.

LARRY: Fucking hell! Was he injured?

GEOFF: No, he seemed fine.

LARRY: Seemed fine?

GEOFF: Well, I didn't get out my stethoscope to give him a full examination!

LARRY: Fucking hell, Geoff. I can't believe you hit a photographer with your car!

GEOFF: He got straight back up and ran after me, so he couldn't have broken anything.

LARRY: Jesus Christ!

GEOFF: Seriously, he was fine.

LARRY: What else did you do? Rob a fucking bank on your way over?

GEOFF: He was fine, OK?

LARRY: Fine.

GEOFF: As I was driving away I was completely filled with fear. I suddenly realized that the money had been on the dashboard when they took the pictures, which made everything look even worse. Then I saw that they were following me. My mind was racing thinking about the headlines, about all the people in my life. I was shaking. I thought about my career. How those few minutes could suddenly eclipse everything that had gone before. All those years of hard work, all the awards, all the programmes, all the good things, Larry, all the things done with good intentions. I started to cry. What would I tell my mother? What was Paul gonna say? I felt completely trapped.

LARRY applauds.

LARRY: Great. That last bit was great. That's exactly what we need. Write it down while it's fresh.

GEOFF: What?

LARRY: Go into Word and write it down.

GEOFF: But…

LARRY: Christ! Move over, let me do it.

LARRY sits at the laptop and writes.

GEOFF: So what do we…

LARRY: Hang on…

LARRY carries on writing.

What was after 'two minutes would eclipse everything'?

GEOFF: What?

LARRY: Dadadadada…two minutes would eclipse everything…

GEOFF: I don't know, I…

LARRY: 'All those years of hard work'! That's it. Great. Magic.

GEOFF: So what are…

LARRY: Ah. Ah. Ah.

He finishes off what he's writing.

Right. So this is the plan. I'm gonna shape this up a little bit and then we need to get you out there for a statement.

GEOFF: A statement?

LARRY: Yes.

GEOFF: I thought you were gonna do that.

LARRY: Me?

GEOFF: Yes. As my representative.

LARRY: Your representative didn't get caught fucking a hoodie in a car.

GEOFF: You can still make the statement.

LARRY: They want you to say sorry.

GEOFF: Say sorry?

LARRY: You *need* to say sorry.

GEOFF: I don't have to say sorry to anyone!

LARRY: Yes, you do.

GEOFF: What? Sorry to the photographers? For not posing for close-ups in my moment of terror?

LARRY: No. To the people!

GEOFF: To the people?

LARRY: Yes, to the people!

GEOFF: Oh yes. To the people. Of course…Yes, I'm so sorry everyone that you're forced to read those dumbfuck newspapers every day!

LARRY: This isn't helping!

GEOFF: No sincerely. I'm so sorry that you're too stupid to care about anything substantial in your lives!
So fucking sorry to hit you over the head with Iraq and global warming when all you care about is where Geoffrey Hammond puts his cock!
So fucking sorry everyone for what fucking shallow cunts you all are!

LARRY: Fine. Do it Geoff. We don't need the people anyway, do we?…

GEOFF: No, fuck em!

LARRY: Oh, hang on…who watches the news?

GEOFF: What?

LARRY: Who watches the news?

GEOFF: What do you mean?

LARRY: The people. The people watch the news. Who buys books?

GEOFF: Shut up, Larry.

LARRY: No, seriously. Who buys books?

GEOFF: You are such a patronising wanker, Larry, do you know that?

LARRY: Who buys books, Geoff? Cats? Dogs? Llamas? Antelopes?
The people. The people buy books. Who watches documentaries?

GEOFF: I get the message.

LARRY: Who watches documentaries?

GEOFF: THE PEOPLE. THE FUCKING PEOPLE!

LARRY: Yes, the fucking people. So go ahead. Tell the fucking people to go fuck themselves!
But if you want any kind of career tomorrow, you need to apologise!

GEOFF: This isn't a walk in the park, Larry. I can't do it. I physically can't, OK?

LARRY: So what's the alternative?

GEOFF: I don't know.

LARRY: They need to see you! They need to know you give a fuck!

Silence.

OK, compromise – I go out and make the speech, you record a video apology.

GEOFF: Is this really…

LARRY: They need to see you! I've got a camera. We'll record it here and then we'll post it online.

GEOFF: I'm not sure.

LARRY: Look, this is me at my most cooperative. I will only make the speech, if you record the apology.

GEOFF: OK, fine.

LARRY: Great. So once it's done, we have 24 hours to secure either an exclusive confession interview or a high profile reality show.

GEOFF: I'm not doing a reality show.

LARRY: Trust me, they're golden ticket back into the hearts of the public.

GEOFF: I'm not sinking that low.

LARRY: They work fucking wonders, baby! Eat a few rats in the jungle and the public forgive you anything from shoplifting to date rape.

GEOFF: I'm not doing that. That's non-negotiable.

LARRY: We'll discuss that when we get an offer from Kiddiefiddler Island.
For now let's focus on the apology. Not too long, but from the heart. Also we need to get some voices of support. Famous friends, colleagues, your wife…

GEOFF: Elaine?

LARRY: Yes. Let's call her.

GEOFF: What? No!

LARRY: Just a friendly call.

GEOFF: She'll be asleep.

LARRY: She's gonna find out one way or another…

GEOFF: No, Larry. Let's wait.

LARRY: She needs to know!

LARRY gets his phone and starts dialling.

GEOFF: Larry!

GEOFF chases LARRY around the living room trying to grab the phone away from him.

Give me that!

LARRY gets away. Elaine answers the phone.

LARRY: (*To Elaine.*) Oh, hello…just a moment, I have a call for you…please hold…
(*To Geoff.*) It's for you!

GEOFF gives LARRY an evil look, but takes the phone.

GEOFF: Hi bunny. There's a matter…there's something… nothing major…there's something I need to…You've heard?…Yes, that's why I wanted to call you immediately to…Right. I understand…Yes, I understand…Yeah…Yes, I do…Of course I do…Yes.
(*To Larry.*) She wants the divorce moved forward. And I need to have all my things out of the house by Sunday.

LARRY: Let me speak to her.

GEOFF hands him the phone.

Elaine – darling, it's Larry. This must be such a difficult time. Fortunately I have a fantastic opportunity for you! This would be your chance to tell your side of the story. Hello?…Hello?…

LARRY hangs up the phone.

Bitch. We'll try her again later. We can live with the divorce.

GEOFF: What's Paul gonna say?

LARRY: More importantly – what are the papers gonna say? Actually, that's easy. 'Newscaster Sucks Teen in Car'.

GEOFF: I wasn't sucking when they took the pictures.

LARRY: Well, that's some consolation.

GEOFF: I was fingering him on the passenger seat.

LARRY: Jesus Christ! That's what they got? That's what they got the picture of?

GEOFF: Well, no…I…

LARRY: Have you got no fucking shame?

GEOFF: The camera was miles away. They wouldn't have got that. I was just saying…

LARRY: I thought they came running towards you!

GEOFF: By that time we were half-way decent. They didn't get anything really bad or damaging.

LARRY: Are you sure?!

GEOFF: Yes, I don't think they did.

LARRY: You don't think?

GEOFF: They couldn't have. Trust me. I shouldn't have even said anything.

LARRY: OK, fine.

GEOFF: So this video apology. You think it will work?

LARRY: Sure. People still listen to George Michael.

GEOFF: I guess you're right.

LARRY: Michael Barrymore's working, John Leslie, Gary Glitter…

GEOFF: Fuck off!

LARRY: We could book you all together on a little tour. You'll be like the 'Three Tenors' of sex crime.

GEOFF: I'm not a criminal!

LARRY: Well, we might want to consult the dictionary on that one. I have to call Cindy. Start making some notes. This has to be from the heart.

LARRY gets the phone and starts to dial. GEOFF is fiddling with the laptop.

And don't worry about Paul. He'll be fine.

GEOFF: I'm not so sure of that.

LARRY: Well, he must have cheated on you at some point.

GEOFF: What's that supposed to mean?

LARRY: (*On phone.*) Hey Cindy, it's Larry…he's here…yes, reporters everywhere…No, he can't speak. …Look, for now just put 'Mr Hammond would like to ask the media to respect his privacy at this difficult time for him and his family. He appreciates the support from all his fans at a point where this unfortunate incident is contrasted with the joyous release of his autobiography available at Waterstone's priced £14.99.' What do you mean, too much?…Fine. Words to that effect…And then just add something about him working on some documentaries and having his fingers in a number of pies…Shit, actually, don't use that phrase, OK?…I'll call you in an hour…What?…. Oh…We'll check it out, OK…I'll catch you later. Thanks Cindy…Bye.

He hangs up.

GEOFF: What did you mean when you said that he must have cheated on me?

LARRY: Who?

GEOFF: Paul!

LARRY: Oh. I just meant in your situation…Can you see the remote over there? She says you're all over Sky…

GEOFF: What? No, I can't see it.

LARRY: Check the couch.

GEOFF checks the couch.

GEOFF: What do you mean, in my situation?

LARRY: You can hardly expect him to be faithful while you're still married. (*Finds remote.*) Got it. It was on the table.

GEOFF: Why do you say that?

LARRY: Because it was on the table.

GEOFF: No!! Why wouldn't he be faithful?

LARRY: Christ! It's an assumption that would make your life a little easier right now. (*Switches on the TV.*) Ouch, adding ten pounds, adding ten pounds. You know, I have some great contacts in radio.

GEOFF suddenly notices something on TV.

GEOFF: What's that? What are they saying? Turn it up.

LARRY turns up the volume.

TV PRESENTER: (*On TV.*) Stay with us for more live coverage on the Geoffrey Hammond Sex Scandal as it happens. With me now I have media expert and veteran broadcaster Harvey Millner for a look at tomorrow's papers.

GEOFF: God, is he still around?

TV PRESENTER: (*On TV.*) Harvey, what are the papers making of our top story?

GEOFF: I went to Cambridge with him. Such a cunt.

LARRY: Be quiet for a second.

GEOFF: God, he's definitely had some work done.

HARVEY MILLNER: (*On TV.*) Well, I think the focus won't really be on the individual takes on the story, but rather on the pictures that are being printed with it. Geoffrey Hammond has really made a seriously stupid mistake here.

GEOFF: Cunt.

LARRY: Shhh!

HARVEY MILLNER: (*On TV.*) Of course this is exactly the kind of sleaze we've come to expect from his publicist Larry deVries who was recently sacked as talent judge on ITV2's awful reality show 'Make Me An It-Girl'.

LARRY: You're right. He's a cunt.

HARVEY MILLNER: (*On TV.*) But these are by far the most explicit pictures ever to be printed in a national newspaper and I'm sure they will cause a lot of controversy.

LARRY: What?!

TV PRESENTER: (*On TV.*) Yes. The pictures are indeed very explicit. So much in fact that we can't actually show them to you on air right now.

GEOFF: Shit.

LARRY: Fucking hell!

TV PRESENTER: (*On TV.*) Harvey, do think that it is really necessary to present them in this way or have we reached a new low in our celebrity-driven culture by printing images like this in newspapers that are available to anyone without any age restriction?

HARVEY MILLNER: (*On TV.*) Well, as Simon Kester from the Mail said earlier, Geoffrey Hammond is a very public figure, so in a way it's in everyone's interest to present the full facts to the public and give everyone the chance to make up their own minds.

LARRY puts the TV on mute.

LARRY: I thought you said they didn't get anything damaging.

GEOFF: How am I supposed to know? Have you seen the lenses on those cameras? I'm not a technician!

LARRY: You're gonna be a fucking laughing stock!

Geoffrey Hammond with his hand in the cookie jar!
Literally!

GEOFF: OK OK OK. Let's not lose our heads. What can we do
to combat this?

LARRY: I don't know.

GEOFF: You're a problem solver, Larry, let's keep going. What
can we do?

LARRY: You're fucked, Geoff, you're royally fucked!

GEOFF: What can we do Larry? Come on, work with me!
Please.

LARRY: OK. I need to get a better idea of what we're
expecting. I need to visualize it.

GEOFF: Sure, ask me anything you want.

LARRY gets a notepad.

LARRY: OK. In the photograph, how much is he wearing?

GEOFF: Well, he's wearing a T-shirt, but his Jeans are around
his ankles.

LARRY: OK, and you're the same?

GEOFF: No. I'm still wearing my Jeans.

LARRY: Good. So you're fully clothed?

GEOFF: Yes.

LARRY is enthusiastically making notes in full PR mode.

LARRY: Excellent! So they didn't get you naked?

GEOFF: Well, no, but my fly's undone and I've got my penis
out.

LARRY crosses out all the notes he has just made.

LARRY: Right. Where's your head at this point?

GEOFF: It's sort of next to his and…erm…and…

LARRY: And what?

GEOFF: And I…(*Mumbles.*)…s'ear.

LARRY: What?

GEOFF: And I've got my tongue in his ear!

LARRY: Well Yummedy Yum!

GEOFF: Look, this isn't easy for me!

LARRY: I never said it was!

GEOFF: Just cut the sarcasm, OK?

LARRY: Fine. So you're leaning all the way over him to get to his left ear?

GEOFF: No, his right ear.

LARRY: And his legs are over yours?

GEOFF: No, on the dashboard.

LARRY: What? Look, this isn't working. You're gonna have to show me the position you were in.

GEOFF: Fuck off!

LARRY: I don't want a dramatic interpretation. Just roughly, so I know what angle they got.

GEOFF: Is this really necessary?

LARRY: It would really help me to get an idea of the scope of what we're expecting.

GEOFF: Well, alright.

LARRY gets 2 chairs and places them next to each other. He sits down on one of them.

LARRY: Great. OK, so this is your car. Come here, sit down.

GEOFF sits down in the chair next to him.

So I'll be the boy.

GEOFF: OK.

LARRY: No funny business.

GEOFF: Will you cut that out?

LARRY: Sorry.

GEOFF: You're making this very difficult.

LARRY: I'm just trying to lighten it up a little.

GEOFF: Let's just get on with it.

LARRY: Right, so I'm just lying here minding my own business with my pants around my ankles. And where are you?

GEOFF: This is humiliating.

LARRY: In a few hours every household in the country will see this, so you may as well get used to it. Where are you?

GEOFF: Well…I'm kind of here and I'm leaning over him, sort of like this with my right shoulder…and…Oh, I can't do this!

LARRY: Go on, you're doing well!

GEOFF: OK. Well, I've got my head sort of here…

LARRY: Right. And you've got your tongue in my ear…

GEOFF: Yes, tongue in the ear…and then…

LARRY: Your hand prodding deep into my arsehole.

GEOFF: You're taking the fucking piss!

LARRY: Look, do you want me to help you?

GEOFF: Just keep it professional, OK?

LARRY: Fine.

GEOFF: I'm not being uncooperative. You can ask me anything you want.

LARRY: Anything?

GEOFF: Anything at all.

LARRY: OK. How many fingers?

GEOFF: What?!

LARRY: You heard me, Geoff, how many fingers?

GEOFF: That's none of your fucking business!

LARRY: It is now! How many fingers?

GEOFF: How dare you, Larry! Christ, I knew you were going to gloat when I came begging for your help, but this is fucking ridiculous! I have been voted broadcaster of the year for 3 consecutive years!!! Fuck! Do you want both of our careers to go down the toilet?

LARRY: HOW MANY FUCKING FINGERS!??

GEOFF: THREE!

LARRY: Well done. That wasn't so difficult now, was it?

LARRY's phone rings. He looks at the number, but doesn't answer.

It's Paul.

GEOFF: Don't answer it.

LARRY: You should speak to him.

GEOFF: I'll call him later.

LARRY: Come on, Geoff. You have to.

GEOFF: My relationship with Paul has nothing to do with you, Larry. I will decide when I speak to him, is that clear?

LARRY: OK. Fine.

LARRY cancels the call.

GEOFF: Why do you have his number?

LARRY: What?

GEOFF: Why do you have Paul's number?

LARRY: *He* called *me.*

GEOFF: Yes, but you have his number stored in your phone.

LARRY: Yes.

GEOFF: Well, how did you get it?

LARRY: I don't know. I probably asked him for it.

GEOFF: Why do you need Paul's number?

LARRY: To get hold of you. As an emergency contact.

GEOFF: So you'd just contact him in an emergency?

LARRY: Yes. You're being paranoid.

GEOFF: And what would I be paranoid about?

LARRY: Can we drop this?

GEOFF: Have you slept with Paul?

LARRY: What?!

GEOFF: Just answer the question, Larry!

LARRY: Why do you even ask me that?

GEOFF: Yes or No!?

LARRY: Of course I haven't slept with Paul!

GEOFF: Because if you have that would be the meanest, cruellest thing you could ever do to me! Do you understand?

LARRY: Look at me, OK? I have not slept with Paul.

GEOFF: OK.

LARRY: Great.

GEOFF: I'm sorry for…

LARRY: It's fine.

GEOFF: It's just that…

LARRY: It's fine.

GEOFF: OK.

LARRY: (*Looking at TV.*) Hang on, is this the boy?

GEOFF: Yes.

LARRY: Where's the car? Where are…Hang on, where is this?

GEOFF: It's…

LARRY: Is that…He's outside!

GEOFF: What?

LARRY: What the fuck is he doing here?

GEOFF: Shit.

LARRY: The hotel is miles away. How did he get here?

GEOFF: Fuck.

LARRY: Did you…?

GEOFF: Fuck fuck fuck.

LARRY: YOU TOOK HIM WITH YOU?

GEOFF: Well, what could I have done? Throw him to the photographers with his pants down?

LARRY: So you throw him to the national press instead?

GEOFF: I was confused. It all went so quickly.

LARRY: You fucking idiot!

GEOFF: I was gonna drop him off somewhere, but by the time I shook them off, I was almost here. So I let him out at the end of your road. He said he'd wait for the first train.

LARRY: Great!

GEOFF: Well, I couldn't bring him in here, could I?

LARRY: Fucking great.

GEOFF: I was almost refused entry myself!

LARRY: He'll have his own daytime talk show by lunchtime! Did it even occur to you that he might be the one who called them?

GEOFF: Why would he do that?

LARRY: Fame is fame, baby. If he has no other talent he may as well be the boy who got dicked by that guy who used to be on the telly.

GEOFF: Still is.

LARRY: Whatever. Semantics.

GEOFF: Not to me!

LARRY: Give me the remote.

GEOFF gives him the remote. LARRY turns up the volume.

REPORTER: (*On TV.*) Thank you, Valerie. I'm outside the house of celebrity publicist Larry DeVries, best known for his rather short stint as a judge on 'Make Me An It-Girl', who is currently conferring with his client Geoffrey Hammond about our breaking story. We can now reveal that the teenager in question has been identified as 16 year-old Jamie Sullivan, who's been living with his grandparents since his parents passed away in a tragic car accident last year.

LARRY: Great, he had to be a fucking orphan, didn't he?!

REPORTER: (*On TV.*) Oh, and I've just been told that Jamie is available for a quick interview with us now.

LARRY: And it just gets better!

GEOFF: Shut up! Maybe it's not so bad.

REPORTER: (*On TV.*) So if we just…can I…Oh,…sorry about that…sorry, I am now told that we have somehow lost the boy. He seems to have disappeared for the moment. We will try to get him back and hopefully speak to him about tonight's events, but for now back to you, Valerie, in the studio.

LARRY mutes the TV.

GEOFF: Where's he gone?

We suddenly hear the sound of a brick crashing through glass, i.e. the back door to LARRY's house (offstage).

LARRY: What the fuck!?

JAMIE comes running in from the back door in a hysterical frenzy.

JAMIE: I'm sorry! I'm sorry! I couldn't take it anymore!!!! I'm sorry! I thought you wouldn't let me in!!!

LARRY: And you didn't wanna knock just on the off chance?

JAMIE: I'm so sorry! I'll pay for it! Here…I've got a hundred quid in cash on me!

He gets out the money.

LARRY: I wonder where you got that from.

JAMIE: You're angry, aren't you?

LARRY: No.

JAMIE: I can tell you're angry from the way you're looking at me! I'm soooo sorry! I didn't know what to do. I panicked! I just needed to get away! Please don't be angry with me! I really didn't know what to do!!! I just lost it…Don't throw me out!

JAMIE cries.

LARRY: Jesus Christ.

We hear the voice of a reporter coming from the back door.

REPORTER VOICE: (*Off.*) Hello? Jamie? Could we have a quick word?

LARRY: Stay here.

LARRY goes to the other room to speak to the reporter.

(*Off.*) Excuse me, sir, would you mind waiting at the front door please? Jamie is a little overwhelmed by it all. He needs to have a few moments to himself. As I've said, we'll have a statement for you within the hour, OK?

GEOFF: Are you alright?

JAMIE: (sobbing) Yeah. I've just…found it all really hard.

GEOFF: Yeah, me too.

JAMIE: Are they gonna print…that?…In the papers?

GEOFF: I think so. Yes.

JAMIE: Sorry, this is just really difficult…

JAMIE cries again.

GEOFF: Come here, Jamie.

JAMIE goes to GEOFF. They hug. LARRY enters and stares at the hugging in disbelief.

Larry, this is Jamie. (*Pause.*) What?

LARRY: No, carry on. I'm enjoying how much you've learnt from your mistakes.

GEOFF and JAMIE stop hugging. JAMIE is slowly coming out of his hysteria.

JAMIE: I'm really sorry about your door. I hope you're not angry with me. (*Cries.*)

LARRY: No. It's fine.

JAMIE: I can give you some money.

LARRY: Really. It's fine.

JAMIE: Thank you.

GEOFF: Do want anything, Jamie? A cup of tea or something?

JAMIE: No, I'm alright, thanks.

GEOFF: Are you sure? It's not a problem.

JAMIE: Really? Well, I'd love a hot chocolate.

GEOFF: Of course. Larry, do you have any hot chocolate?

LARRY: What?

GEOFF: Jamie would like a hot chocolate.

LARRY: Oh. Right. And anything for you, Mother Goose?

GEOFF: Stop it, he's seriously upset. Come here, Jamie, sit on the sofa.

JAMIE sits on the sofa.

JAMIE: Thank you.

GEOFF: How are you feeling?

JAMIE: A bit better. I still can't believe it. I've always wanted to be on the telly, but not like this. It's horrible.

GEOFF: Yeah, I understand.

Silence.

LARRY: Hang on, what did you just say?

JAMIE: What?

LARRY: Did you just say you've always wanted to be on TV?

51

JAMIE: Yeah.

LARRY: Been a dream of yours, has it?

JAMIE: A little bit, yeah.

LARRY: To be noticed. To be known. To have your fifteen minutes.

JAMIE: I guess.

LARRY: That's interesting.

GEOFF: Larry…

LARRY: That's interesting, isn't it, Geoff?

GEOFF: Larry, no…

LARRY: What a nice little coincidence this must be for you.

JAMIE: What?

LARRY: You found your ticket, didn't you?

GEOFF: Larry, please…

LARRY: Your ticket out of Butt-fuck-nowhere.

JAMIE: What do you mean?

LARRY: Who's paying you? The *Mail*? The *Sun*? The *Mirror*?

JAMIE: Nobody.

GEOFF: Larry, stop it!

LARRY: How much are you getting? Ten grand? Twenty? Thirty? Huh?

JAMIE: I don't know what you're talking about.

GEOFF: Lay off, Larry. For Christ's sake! The boy is clean!

LARRY: Or doesn't it take that much for you to spread your little legs for any random stranger that comes your way?

GEOFF: Larry!

LARRY: Well, let me tell you this. No matter how many people recognise you in the street or tell you how brilliant you are at having no talent whatsoever, nothing's ever gonna replace Mummy and Daddy giving you that fucking hug before bedtime. Nothing's even gonna get close to scratching that itch, do you understand me?

GEOFF: For fuck's sake, Larry. He's an innocent young boy!

LARRY: Innocent young boys play with Nintendo, not with cock! What are you getting for this, tell me!

JAMIE: NOTHING!!! I'VE DONE NOTHING WRONG! NOBODY'S OFFERING ME ANYTHING! I'm fucking scared and I didn't know where to go. I'm not working for any newspaper and nobody's giving me any money. I don't want any fucking money, I just wanna get out of this. Why would I come here if I'd done anything wrong? You have to believe me! I'm just fucking scared!

The atmosphere relaxes.

LARRY: (*To Geoff.*) You're right, Geoff. He is clean. Was that two hot chocolates?

GEOFF: You're a fucking bastard, Larry.

LARRY: I'll take that as a yes.

GEOFF: I'll get it for you, Jamie.

GEOFF goes to the kitchen. JAMIE is still very emotional.

LARRY: I'm sorry. It was the only way.

JAMIE: I know.

LARRY walks over to the desk. JAMIE goes over to him and puts his arms around him. LARRY pushes him away.

LARRY: (*Stern.*) Not while he's in the house!

Lights. End of Act One.

Act Two

Flashback. A layby, GEOFF's car, a few hours earlier. We hear the opening bars to the Etta James song 'At Last'.

Lights up. GEOFF and JAMIE are sitting in the car singing along to 'At Last', which is coming from the car radio. They are sharing a bottle of wine and are slightly tipsy..

GEOFF & JAMIE: (*Singing.*) 'At Last, my love has come along da da da da da da da…'

> *JAMIE turns down the music and kisses GEOFF, but then pulls away.*

GEOFF: You're nervous.

JAMIE: Yeah.

GEOFF: Have you never…

JAMIE: No, I have.

GEOFF: Are you alright?

JAMIE: Yeah.

GEOFF: We don't have to rush anything.

JAMIE: Thanks.

GEOFF: Do you like this kind of music?

JAMIE: It's alright.

GEOFF: Sure?

JAMIE: Yeah, my Dad used to listen to this sort of stuff.

> *Silence.*

GEOFF: Do you have a boyfriend?

JAMIE: I dunno. Sort of.

GEOFF: A sort of boyfriend?

JAMIE: Yeah.

GEOFF: A girlfriend?

JAMIE: No. It's complicated.

GEOFF: I see.

JAMIE: Do you have a boyfriend?

GEOFF: Oh. Well, erm…Yes.

JAMIE: Oh. Right.

GEOFF: And a wife.

> *There is a moment of silence. Then they suddenly burst out laughing.*
> *JAMIE kisses him again. This time longer. They stop. It's all slightly*
> *awkward.*

So you didn't tell me what you want to study.

JAMIE: I don't know. Something…clever.

GEOFF: What are you good at?

> *JAMIE smiles flirtatiously.*

Apart from kissing random strangers.

JAMIE: Random celebrity strangers.

GEOFF: Yes, random celebrity strangers.

JAMIE: I like Geography.

GEOFF: You wanna study Geography?

JAMIE: Dunno, might take the fun out of it.

GEOFF: You should give it a go.

JAMIE: What could I do with it though?

GEOFF: I don't know. You could be an explorer or a lecturer or a researcher or something. See where it takes you. What do you want to be when…

GEOFF stops himself.

JAMIE: When I grow up?

GEOFF: I didn't mean…

JAMIE: It's fine.

GEOFF: OK.

JAMIE: I wanna be famous.

GEOFF laughs.

GEOFF: Famous?

JAMIE: Yeah, like you.

GEOFF: Famous for what?

JAMIE: Dunno, just famous. Do something that everyone loves you for.

GEOFF: That's not being famous.

JAMIE: You don't like it?

GEOFF: It's OK.

JAMIE: I think it would suit me.

GEOFF: Do you?

JAMIE: Yeah.

GEOFF: You know, when I was about your age, I got my first article published in a local newspaper.

JAMIE: Really?

GEOFF: Yeah. It was so exciting. It was only a small column, but I spent hours in my room perfecting the words. I remember my mother cutting it out of the paper and showing everyone who came over.

I always knew I wanted to be a journalist. I used to think this world was so glamorous. If I'd known then that I would be reading the news on television one day and I'd be travelling around the globe, meeting all these famous people...I would have thought that to be the most exhilarating thing in the world.

And then I achieved it. And I discovered that reading the news wasn't as exciting as being a rock star or a world leader or the founder of a human rights movement.

Reading the news wasn't as exciting as making the news.

So I started to miss the times when I was writing for that local newspaper. When I was hungry for something. But suddenly it felt so far away. And I thought 'Wow, I did that once. I couldn't do that now.' And that's when I realised that fame is not as good as achievement. Never will be. (*Silence.*) Sorry, I'm boring you.

JAMIE: No, it's interesting.

GEOFF: You know what else is interesting?

JAMIE: What?

GEOFF: I need to go for a slash.

JAMIE laughs.

Wait here. I'll be right back.

GEOFF gives JAMIE a quick kiss, gets out of the car and closes the door behind him. JAMIE waits until he is out of sight and then makes a phone call.

JAMIE: (*on the phone.*) Hey...I'm in his car...He's gone for a pee...I can't do it...Seriously, I can't. He's being really...I know...I know (*sighs.*)...I...yeah...yeah...I know...OK... (*sighs.*)...We're here now. I think they followed us. OK...OK...I have to go.

JAMIE hangs up. GEOFF comes back. He opens the door and gets out his wallet. He takes out a hundred pounds in cash and hands it to JAMIE. JAMIE doesn't take it.

GEOFF: Here.

JAMIE: I can't take that.

GEOFF: For Geography. Take it.

JAMIE takes the money. GEOFF gets back into the car and closes the door. They stare at each other intensely for a moment.

Well, aren't you gonna say thank you?

The continue to stare at each other. Lights fade to black as 'for you are mine at last' – the last line of the song – plays.

SCENE 2

LARRY's house, living room. LARRY is at the computer. After a few moments JAMIE enters from the kitchen wearing a cardboard party hat and holding a bottle of Jack Daniels. He has been drinking, but isn't fully drunk. He blows into a squawker blowout that you would find at a child's birthday party, which makes a loud noise.

LARRY: Fuck!!

JAMIE: Made you jump!

LARRY: What the fuck are you doing?

JAMIE: I found a box of party supplies.

LARRY: You almost gave me a fucking heart attack!

JAMIE: Where's Geoff?

LARRY: He's writing his thing.

JAMIE: I thought you were writing that.

LARRY: No, he insisted. Put that back.

JAMIE: Put what back?

LARRY: The bottle. All of it. But mainly the bottle.

JAMIE: Why?

LARRY: Because you shouldn't be drinking.

JAMIE: It's a stressful time.

LARRY: What?

JAMIE: It's a stressful time. People drink in stressful times.

LARRY: Well, you shouldn't be.

JAMIE: Because I'm too young?

LARRY: Yes…No! You just shouldn't.

JAMIE: Too young…*to drink.*

 Silence.

 This is like a lock-in in a really fancy bar in Shoreditch.

LARRY: No, it's not.

JAMIE: Like an exclusive party that only we're invited to. Can I get a cuddle?

LARRY: No.

 LARRY goes back to the computer and ignores him. JAMIE sneaks up to him and blows the squawker blowout in his face. LARRY slaps him in the face.

JAMIE: Oww!

LARRY: What the fuck are you playing at?

JAMIE: You can't fucking hit me like that!

LARRY: Keep your voice down!

JAMIE: If you want me to keep my voice down, don't fucking hit me like that!

LARRY: I told you exactly how we needed to play this.

JAMIE: I had to improvise. When he started the car they all went ape-shit!

LARRY: You keep them waiting for an hour and a half, of course they're gonna go ape-shit!

JAMIE: It was fucking difficult, alright?

Silence. JAMIE lies down on the couch and takes his hoodie off.

Hit me again and I'll tell him everything.

LARRY: What?

JAMIE: I will. I'll fucking run upstairs and tell him everything!

LARRY grabs JAMIE by his T-shirt and lifts him up.

LARRY: You listen to me. If you even say one… (*He spots the autograph on Jamie's arm.*) What the fuck is that?

JAMIE: He gave me his autograph.

LARRY: What?

JAMIE: He gave me his autograph.

LARRY: Why?

JAMIE: My sister likes him on the telly.

LARRY: It's on your arm.

JAMIE: I was gonna photocopy it for her.

LARRY: Then it's not even a real autograph.

JAMIE: So she's easily pleased. What's the fucking problem?

LARRY: You weren't meant to piss around getting his autograph. You had a fucking job to do!

JAMIE: And I did it, didn't I?

LARRY drops JAMIE back on the couch and takes the bottle of Jack Daniels back to the kitchen. JAMIE sulks. LARRY comes back with a video camera and a tripod and starts to set them up.

What are you doing?

LARRY: I'm setting up the camera.

JAMIE: I wanna go on holiday.

LARRY: Then you should go on holiday.

JAMIE: I wanna go with you.

LARRY: That's not possible.

JAMIE: If we did go on holiday, where would we go?

LARRY: I don't know.

JAMIE: What's the best holiday you've ever been on?

LARRY: I can't remember.

JAMIE: Come on, you must remember one.

LARRY: No.

JAMIE: They can't have been very good if you can't remember
a single holiday you've been on.

LARRY: OK. Fine. When I thirteen my parents took me and
my sister to Switzerland.

JAMIE: Switzerland?

LARRY: Yes.

JAMIE: That's the best holiday you've ever been on?

LARRY: Yes.

JAMIE: Why?

LARRY: I remember us all getting on.

Silence.

JAMIE: I did it for you, you know.

LARRY: I didn't force you.

JAMIE: No, but you asked me.

LARRY: And you said yes. You said you were fine doing it.

JAMIE: Yeah, it sounded fine from how you described it.

LARRY: Things just didn't go to plan.

JAMIE: No. The way he behaved was different. Weird.

LARRY: What do you mean, weird?

JAMIE: Kind of unpredictable.

LARRY: He didn't hurt you, did he?

JAMIE: Oh no, he was really friendly.

LARRY: Good.

JAMIE: Sort of…affectionate.

LARRY: Affectionate?

JAMIE: Well, polite I mean.

LARRY: Polite.

JAMIE: Yes.

LARRY: Affectionate and polite, those are two different things.

JAMIE: Just the way he speaks and his manners.

LARRY: Right.

JAMIE: And the way he uses his hands.

LARRY: What was this? A fucking candle-lit dinner?

JAMIE: No.

LARRY: You got fingered by an old guy in a car. You make it sound like a snake-charming ritual!

JAMIE: He's in really good shape. He goes swimming twice a week.

LARRY: He told you he goes swimming?

JAMIE: He told me lots of different stuff. He has these great stories.

LARRY: Oh, I'm sure.

JAMIE: He was really interested in what I had to say.

LARRY: Because he wanted to have sex with you.

JAMIE: No, he was being really sincere.

LARRY: Because he wanted to have sex with you. You're sixteen. Older guys will say things in order to have sex with you.

JAMIE: Will they?

He stares at LARRY. Silence.

LARRY: Are you trying to make me jealous?

JAMIE: Oh no, sorry. Was I making you jealous?

LARRY: No, I was just asking if that's what you were trying.

JAMIE: There's nothing to be worried about.

LARRY: I'm not worried either.

JAMIE: Well, if you were, you wouldn't have to be. Compared to him you're just so…

LARRY: Can we not have this conversation?

JAMIE: No, I want to say this.

LARRY: Look, I know what you're going to say and you really don't…

JAMIE: I just want to say that you're a lot…

LARRY: Yes…

JAMIE: …different to Geoff.

LARRY: Different?

JAMIE: Yeah. Completely different.

LARRY: Different. Great.

Silence. JAMIE takes out his phone and looks at it.

JAMIE: Do you remember this?

LARRY: What?

JAMIE: This.

JAMIE shows him his phone.

LARRY: You have my photo on your phone?!

JAMIE: Yeah.

LARRY: Are you fucking retarded?

JAMIE: I like it.

LARRY: For fuck's sake! Give me that!

JAMIE: Fine! I'll delete it. Jesus!

LARRY: Fucking hell.

JAMIE: You're playing with his life.

LARRY: Oh, spare me the melodrama, will you!

JAMIE: It's true though.

LARRY: I know what's best for him.

JAMIE: Public humiliation?

LARRY: I created an opportunity.

JAMIE: It's not fair on him.

LARRY: Oh, was he forced to have sex with you? Did you put a gun to his head? He put himself in this situation because he is weak. All we've done is we've chosen to point it out.

JAMIE: He didn't have a say in it though.

LARRY: Look, we just need him to take responsibility and apologise. Once he's done that everything will be back to normal.

JAMIE: I don't want to do it anymore.

LARRY: It's too late. I need you, Jamie.

JAMIE sighs.

I'll take you on holiday.

JAMIE: I don't wanna go to Switzerland.

LARRY: We don't have to go to fucking Switzerland, we can go wherever you like. OK?

Silence.

JAMIE: Do you love me, Larry?

LARRY: What?

JAMIE: Do you love me?

Silence. GEOFF enters.

GEOFF: I'm ready.

JAMIE: Larry's set up the camera.

GEOFF: I can see.

JAMIE: Looks good, doesn't it?

GEOFF: Indeed.

The room has been turned into a mini TV studio. JAMIE goes to the kitchen.

Over here?

LARRY: Yeah.

GEOFF: I borrowed one of your shirts.

LARRY: Fine.

GEOFF: I feel like I should wear a tie or something.

LARRY: No, the more informal the better.

GEOFF: You think this is alright?

GEOFF indicates his clothes.

LARRY: Yeah, it's fine. Sit down so I can check the light.

LARRY adjusts the camera angle. JAMIE re-enters with the bottle of Jack Daniels. He takes a swig.

JAMIE: This is sooo exciting!

LARRY: Put that back.

GEOFF: Oh, give me some of that!

JAMIE gives GEOFF the bottle. He takes a swig. LARRY ignores it.

JAMIE: This is like being on a real movie set!

LARRY: Yes, sure, it's exactly like that.

JAMIE: You're the director and Geoff's like James Bond.

GEOFF laughs.

GEOFF: James Bond. That's sweet.

LARRY rolls his eyes.

JAMIE: Do the catchphrase!

GEOFF: Which one?

JAMIE: Like when he introduces himself.

GEOFF: No, which Bond?

JAMIE: Daniel Craig.

GEOFF: I don't really know what he sounds like.

JAMIE: Which one can you do?

GEOFF: Roger Moore.

JAMIE: Who?

GEOFF: The name's Bond. James Bond.

GEOFF lifts his eyebrow, makes his hand into a gun and crosses his arms. JAMIE loves it.

JAMIE: And I'm the baddie. 'So, Mister Bond, I've been expecting you.'

GEOFF: 'Vodka Martini. Shaken, not…'

LARRY: OK, can we stop this for a moment?

JAMIE and GEOFF giggle.

GEOFF: OK, OK, OK…serious.

GEOFF tries to compose himself, but is still smirking.

LARRY: Now we're gonna go for a test run, but I'll record anyway just in case there's anything we can use, OK?

GEOFF: Sure.

LARRY: Are you clear about what you're saying?

GEOFF: Yes.

LARRY: Shall I have a quick look over it?

GEOFF: I think 30 years of journalism just about qualify me for writing my own statement, thank you very much.

LARRY: Fine. You ready for a take?

GEOFF: Yes, let's go.

LARRY: Great.

JAMIE: Oh, can I do the clapperboard?

LARRY: No.

JAMIE: Please.

LARRY: We don't need one. And we're rolling in five, four, three…

JAMIE: Please. I've always wanted to do the clapperboard.

LARRY: Could you just shut up for five minutes please?

GEOFF: Oh come on, let him do the clapperboard if he wants.

LARRY: I don't believe this.

JAMIE: Yeah, can I?

GEOFF: Let him do it, Larry.

LARRY: I don't have a fucking clapperboard!

JAMIE: I can use something else.

GEOFF: Do you have one of those big wooden barbeque things that look like a pair of scissors?

LARRY: What are you talking about?

GEOFF: You know, it's big and made out of wood and you turn the meat with it on the barbeque.

JAMIE: Tongs.

GEOFF: Tongs! Yes, that's right. Tongs. That's what they're called. Do you have any?

LARRY: No, I don't have any barbeque tongs.

GEOFF: Oven gloves?

LARRY: What?

GEOFF: He can just put them on and slap his hands together.

LARRY: Is this really necessary?

GEOFF: Oh, come on. It'll be a bit of fun.

LARRY: Yes, because that's what this should be. A bit of fun. A bit of fucking fun!

GEOFF: Oh, don't be such a spoilsport, Larry!

LARRY: In the kitchen. To the right of the oven.

JAMIE: Brilliant!

JAMIE runs to the kitchen. GEOFF notices a book on the desk.

GEOFF: What's this?

LARRY: What?

GEOFF: GCSE Geography. How did that get here?

LARRY: I'm diversifying my interests.

GEOFF: (*Suspiciously.*) How did this get here, Larry?

LARRY: My nephew left it here at the weekend.

GEOFF: Your nephew?

LARRY: Yes, I told you my sister's getting a divorce.

GEOFF: What's his name?

LARRY: What?

GEOFF: What's his name?

LARRY: Jason.

GEOFF: So if I opened this book, the name I'd see written in the front would be Jason, yes?

LARRY: Yes.

There is a moment of silence. He stares at LARRY. Then he opens the book and looks inside.

GEOFF: (*Reading.*) Jason Fenwick, Year 10.

LARRY: Yes. Can we get on with this now?

GEOFF: Sure.

JAMIE comes back with the oven gloves. LARRY switches the camera on.

JAMIE: Got them.

LARRY: And we're rolling.

JAMIE: Geoffrey Hammond sex scandal confession take one!

JAMIE slaps the oven gloves together and blows in his squawker blowout.

LARRY: And action!

GEOFF: Good evening. My name is Geoffrey Hammond.

A phone makes a strange noise.

What's that?

JAMIE has received a text message.

JAMIE: My friend Nat just saw me on TV. She wants to know if she can come over.

LARRY: No, she can't.

JAMIE sighs in disappointment.

LARRY: Let's go again.

JAMIE: Geoffrey Hammond sex scandal confession take two!

Once again JAMIE slaps the oven gloves together and blows in his squawker blowout.

GEOFF: Good evening.

LARRY: Hang on, why do you keep saying good evening?

GEOFF: That's just what I say.

LARRY: It's not even evening.

GEOFF: Well, when will this be shown?

LARRY: I don't know. Just don't say anything that limits us to a certain time.

GEOFF: OK.

LARRY: Rolling.

JAMIE: Geoffrey Hammond sex scandal confession take three!

JAMIE slaps the oven gloves together and blows in his squawker blowout.

GEOFF: Hello. My name is Geoffrey Hammond. Every day I speak to you and inform you about the world's events. Matters of life and death, joy and sorrow, hope and disappointment. Tonight I speak to you on a different matter.

As you may know, I was part of an unfortunate incident earlier today. But I have trust in the British public. I have trust that you can see the person beyond these events.

LARRY: Stop. Cut!

GEOFF: What?

LARRY: Is that how you're gonna do it?

GEOFF: Like what?

LARRY: Were you just running the words or is that the way you're actually gonna do it?

GEOFF: What's wrong with it?

LARRY: Just the style and the intonation. It's so sterile.

GEOFF: Sterile?

LARRY: Yes, like a newsreader.

GEOFF: I am a newsreader!

JAMIE: I thought it was really good.

LARRY: Oh, here we go!

GEOFF: Thank you, Jamie.

JAMIE: Really professional.

LARRY: There needs to be more of an emotional investment.

GEOFF: Will you at least let me finish?

LARRY: I really think that…

GEOFF: Just let me finish, OK?

LARRY: Fine!

JAMIE: Do we need the clapperboard again?

LARRY: No.

GEOFF: I'm just gonna carry on. We'll edit it together.

GEOFF clears his voice.

I have trust that you can see the person beyond these
events. The person you have known for years. The familiar
face in your living room.
Everyone one of us has a side that we don't want put under
a microscope. It doesn't mean that our other sides are no
longer true because of it.

LARRY: Jesus Christ!

GEOFF: What?

LARRY: It's not the Queen's fucking Christmas Speech!

GEOFF: What do you mean?

LARRY: What's all that face in your living room thing? That's
just creepy!

GEOFF: I'm making a point.

LARRY: What, that we all have a fucking song in our hearts?
Give me a break!

GEOFF: If I'd been caught with a woman, nobody would give
a fuck!

LARRY: Oh, boo-hoo. Poor little gayboy! What do you want
me to do? A little protest march around the living room?

GEOFF: I'm scared. What the fuck is gonna happen to me,
Larry?

JAMIE: Shall I call my sister?

GEOFF & LARRY: What?!

JAMIE: She does Tarot cards. She could do your cards.

LARRY: Shut up, Jamie.

JAMIE: No, she's really good. She even predicted the seven eleven attacks.

GEOFF: Thanks Jamie, but…

LARRY: Seven Eleven are a chain of food stores in America.

GEOFF: I wanna do the end of this.

LARRY: What's the point?

GEOFF: Turn the fucking camera on!

LARRY: Fine. Knock yourself out.

LARRY turns on the camera. GEOFF sits up straight and clears his voice again.

GEOFF: (*To camera.*) How you choose to judge me is up to you. And I will also take some time to reflect on these events. As a newsreader it is my responsibility to retain a neutral relationship with my viewers. And therefore I have decided that it would not be appropriate to apologise to you today.

LARRY: What?!

GEOFF: Instead I have chosen to make my apologies in private to the individuals affected by my actions. I hope that you will respect my privacy whilst I try to rebuild my life with some sort of dignity. They say time is a great healer and I plan to find out. Good night.

LARRY: What the fuck are you doing?

GEOFF: I've decided. I'm not doing it, Larry. I'm not apologising.

LARRY: Oh yes you fucking are!

GEOFF: I'm not crucifying myself on national television.

LARRY: You are the most arrogant selfish pompous cunt I have ever…

LARRY's phone rings. He picks up.

LARRY: Yes. What?!…Oh, hi Cindy…Really?…That's fantastic. What are the dates?…Excellent. We'll discuss it and get back to you, OK?…great, thanks Cindy! I'm sure he will be. Bye.

LARRY hangs up.

It's an offer.

GEOFF: What is it?

LARRY: Now I want you to let go of all your prejudices.

GEOFF: For fuck's sake, Larry, what is it?

LARRY: Reality show. Prime Time. Channel Five.

GEOFF: No way!

LARRY: I've not even told you the premise yet!

GEOFF: What's the premise?

LARRY: Celebrity Dental Practice.

JAMIE: Wicked!

GEOFF: What?

LARRY: Five celebrities running a dental practice with hilarious consequences.

GEOFF: But I'm not a dentist.

LARRY: They'll send you on a course!

GEOFF: I'm not that desperate.

LARRY: Yes, you are!

GEOFF: I still have a career!

LARRY: That's because the people who can fire you are still in bed.

GEOFF: I have been voted broadcaster of the year for 3 consecutive years. I get hundreds of letters every week.

LARRY: So does Charles Manson, Geoff. And that includes wedding proposals.

GEOFF: There must be another way!

LARRY: Don't you get it? You're disposable. Nobody needs to give you a second chance.

GEOFF: We can sort this out. Get Elaine involved. Do a photo session.

LARRY: They already have the photo they want.

GEOFF: We could educate people. Challenge prejudices.

LARRY: Yes, Geoffrey Hammond, the great gay role model. In the closet, married to a woman and pays teenagers for sex! That's really gonna challenge prejudices, isn't it?

GEOFF: Change people's perceptions.

LARRY: You have one minute to sit at that table and apologise to the public or I open my front door to the national press!

Silence.

GEOFF: Fuck you, Larry. I quit.

LARRY: You quit?

GEOFF: Yes, I quit.

LARRY: Fine.

GEOFF: Fine?

LARRY: Yeah. Fine.

Silence.

You know what the great thing is about journalism, Geoff?

GEOFF: What, Larry?

LARRY: There's always two sides to every story. (*Beat.*)
Jamie, have you ever had your own publicist?

JAMIE: Erm…no.

LARRY: Someone to help you when the going got tough, when
you needed something to be put right. You know, a bit
like…a *Dad*, but different.

JAMIE: I don't know what you mean.

LARRY: How would you feel about addressing the nation live
on television?

JAMIE: What? Me?

GEOFF: Don't listen to him, Jamie. He's crazy.

LARRY: Could you not interrupt when I'm conferring with a
potential client, Geoff? It's very rude.

GEOFF: We have to stick together on this, Jamie!

LARRY: Why? Were you planning on letting him tell his
side of the story? Oh hang on,…that's not really in your
interest, is it?

GEOFF: He's just trying to manipulate you, Jamie!

LARRY: Or maybe I care. Maybe I want to give you the
chance to let people know how you feel.

GEOFF: Oh this is bullshit. You know precisely that it's my
story they want.

LARRY: No, Geoff. It's the most charming trait of the British
people. They always side with the underdog. He's got it all.
Troubled past, dead parents… Jamie, daytime TV is gonna
be your oyster!

GEOFF: Of course. You should give him dancing lessons and put him in Billy fucking Elliot.

LARRY: Oh my God, you're jealous!

GEOFF: I'm not jealous. This is ridiculous!

LARRY: You're jealous of a young kid who just got violently raped.

JAMIE: What?

GEOFF: He did not get violently raped!

LARRY: He could have done though, couldn't he? All alone with you in that car in the middle of nowhere.

GEOFF: Don't you dare, Larry.

LARRY: Nobody's saying that you did. But maybe there could be a misunderstanding in the papers for a few days.

GEOFF: There were photographers there. Witnesses!

LARRY: Yes, one of whom could have heard a cry or a scream. You know, something that could turn out just to have been a stray dog a few days later.

JAMIE: Stop talking like this!

GEOFF: They're not gonna buy that. They saw the money. They're gonna think he's nothing but a lowlife rentboy turning tricks in the street.

LARRY: You hear this, Jamie? A lowlife rentboy turning tricks in the street. Is that how you want people to see you? That's what Geoff thinks.

Did you know that 28 per cent of all teenagers who lose a parent at an early age are likely to go into prostitution, Geoff?

GEOFF: Is that true?

LARRY: No, but it looks great in print. There he was, trying to turn things around, go to university, make something of himself. When along comes Geoffrey Hammond, making him earn the money for his education. And when he refuses, well, bad luck, Jamie…

GEOFF: You're a backstabbing cunt, Larry.

LARRY: It's the perfect redemption story. The boy next door who got on the wrong path is coming home. Well, not literally next door, more like a few streets down where the big council estate is. So what do you think, Jamie?

JAMIE: I..I can't…do this. Sorry…

LARRY: If I was your publicist, me and you would have to spend a lot of time together, travel together, that kind of thing. You understand?

JAMIE: Yeah. I just…

LARRY: We need to make sure that you get out of this situation unharmed. So that the public…*and your sister and your grandparents* understand that you are the victim in all of this.

JAMIE: I'm not really sure.

LARRY: I'd hate for your family not to get the protection they deserve!

JAMIE: OK…OK…I'll do it.

GEOFF: Jamie…

LARRY: Excellent.

JAMIE: I'm sorry.

JAMIE goes to the bedroom. He can't look GEOFF in the eyes.

GEOFF: Jamie!

LARRY: Each man for himself, Geoff. You can't blame Jamie for looking out for his own interests.

GEOFF: I hope you burn in hell, Larry!

LARRY: And on that note, Geoff, it is with regret that I accept your resignation.

GEOFF: I can get myself a new publicist.

LARRY: At 6 in the morning? Good luck!

GEOFF: So I'll wait a few hours. It won't make a difference.

LARRY: By which time Jamie will be on GMTV talking about how you plied him with alcohol and how you couldn't take no for an answer. Oh, and don't forget, our contract ties you to me exclusively for another week and a half!

GEOFF: Fuck you!

LARRY: I suggest you call yourself a cab.

Loud banging on the door. The press is getting rowdy.

(*Shouting.*) Yes! Gentlemen! Please! He'll be right with you.

Silence.

GEOFF: Fine. I'll do what you say. Let's just get it over with.

LARRY: Good boy.

LARRY takes the phone from GEOFF's hands and dials a number.

Cindy?…Call Channel Five. We're accepting the offer…. Thanks.

LARRY hangs up. He gets a pen and notepad and throws it at GEOFF.

You will be addressing this crowd in five minutes with the following words. Write this down.

GEOFF takes the pad and pen and does as he is told.

'Dear friends, colleagues and respected viewers,
I have made a terrible mistake. I have betrayed your trust and taken advantage of a vulnerable young person.'

GEOFF: It was consensual. He's not underage!

LARRY: He's still vulnerable though, isn't he?

GEOFF: We're all fucking vulnerable!

LARRY: Just write it down, Geoff.

GEOFF reluctantly continues to write.

'Nothing I can say can make up for the hurt and disappointment I have caused so many people today. I hope that in time you can find it in your hearts to accept my sincerest apology.'
That's it. Short and simple. That's not so hard now, is it?

GEOFF finishes writing the apology. Silence.

GEOFF: Why is this anyone's business?

LARRY: Because it's news, Geoff.

GEOFF: News? Even the word's a joke.
There's nothing *new* about anything anymore. Every story. Every exclusive. Every headline. Everything's a journalist's interpretation of a publicist's reconstruction of actual events. There's no such thing as news anymore. Everything exists to further someone else's interest. For someone to get a slice of the cake.

Silence.

LARRY: Of course. (*Beat.*) But this is just the first time it's bothered you.

Silence.

One minute.

LARRY exits. After a few seconds JAMIE enters.

JAMIE: I'm sorry.

GEOFF: It's OK.

JAMIE: No, I'm…sorry…because…

GEOFF: Because?

JAMIE: About everything.

GEOFF: It's not your fault.

JAMIE: You'll be alright.
You could write a newspaper column again like you used to.

GEOFF: No, I don't think so. I'm gonna lose everything. Do you know what that feels like?

JAMIE: Yeah. I was in the car when it happened.

GEOFF: I know you were.

JAMIE: No. My parents. I was in the car with them when it happened.
It was only in our local paper.

Silence.

GEOFF: Come and lie down.

JAMIE: OK.

JAMIE lies down on the couch. GEOFF takes a blanket and puts it over him. He kisses his forehead. JAMIE closes his eyes and goes to sleep. GEOFF takes his phone and makes a call.

GEOFF: (*Gently.*) Paul?…It's me…Have you…?…Yes…I'm sorry.
Hello?…Can you…Oh, right.
Have *you*…ever cheated on…?…OK.
I have to make a statement and I'll be home in a few hours…
I'm so sorry that I've let you down.
(*Cries.*) I'm sorry…I love you. I love you so much. (*Cries.*)
Paul? Can you…? Can you hear me now?…Can you hear me now?

His phone has died, he fidgets with it for a moment, it becomes clear it's not going to work. He sees JAMIE's phone lying next to him, goes over and takes it. As he turns it on, he sees the picture of LARRY and JAMIE on the phone. Just in that moment JAMIE wakes up. They look at each other, like two rabbits in the headlights.

When was this taken?

JAMIE: I didn't mean to…

GEOFF: When was this taken?

JAMIE: I didn't think it would be like this. I…

GEOFF: Shhh…

GEOFF puts a finger in front of his mouth.

Will you…do something for me? (*Beat.*) Please?

JAMIE: OK.

They hear LARRY coming. GEOFF quickly goes over to JAMIE and whispers something in his ear. JAMIE lies down and pretends to sleep. LARRY enters.

LARRY: Showtime!

GEOFF: Indeed.

LARRY: Go speak to your people, Geoff.

GEOFF: Yes.

LARRY: Think of this as a new chapter. Walk your Via Dolorosa to media redemption.

GEOFF: Yes, Larry. I will.

LARRY: There's good money in humiliation.

GEOFF: Yes. What's that saying? One man's poison is another man's meat.
Or is it the other way round?

LARRY: You ready?

GEOFF: Yes.

LARRY: Good luck, Geoff.

GEOFF: Thanks.

GEOFF goes to the door.

LARRY: Oh, and Geoff...

GEOFF turns to him in silence.

LARRY: I slept with Paul. When you were in France. He was so fucking easy.

GEOFF doesn't react. He opens the door to a lightning storm of cameras, walks out and closes the door behind him. LARRY looks at JAMIE, who has woken up.

Relax. It's all over.

JAMIE: Yeah.

LARRY: You did well.

JAMIE: Thanks.

LARRY: Go get some sleep.

JAMIE: OK.

LARRY: Come on.

LARRY makes his way to the bedroom. JAMIE gets up from the sofa.

JAMIE: Wait.

LARRY: What?

JAMIE: Can I get that cuddle?

LARRY: Of course.

LARRY goes over to JAMIE and they hug for a moment. JAMIE kisses LARRY on the mouth. In that moment GEOFF suddenly throws the front door wide open to the national press. Cameras flash everywhere taking pictures of LARRY and JAMIE kissing. LARRY is trapped and his face freezes with fear. GEOFF and LARRY's eyes meet. GEOFF smiles.

GEOFF: You're right, Larry! Two sides to every story.

The camera flashes turn into one big intense light that becomes brighter and brighter. The noise from the press gets louder and louder. At full almost blinding brightness we cut to black.

THE END

www.ingramcontent.com/pod-product-compliance
Ingram Content Group UK Ltd.
Pitfield, Milton Keynes, MK11 3LW, UK
UKHW020726280225
455688UK00012B/521

9 781840 029772